The Physical Sciences

ENERGY

Andrew Solway

WAYLAND

First published in 2007 by Wayland

Copyright © Wayland 2007

Wayland
338 Euston Road
London NW1 3BH

Wayland
Level 17/207 Kent Street
Sydney, NSW 2000

Editor: Vicky Brooker

British Library Cataloguing in Publication Data
Solway, Andrew
Energy. - (The physical sciences)
1. Force and energy - Juvenile literaturen
I. Title
531.6
ISBN-13: 9780750250146

Printed in China

Wayland is a division of Hachette Children's Books.

The website addresses (URLs) included in this book were valid at the time of going to press. However, because of the nature of the Internet, it is possible that some addresses may have changed, or sites may have changed or closed down since publication. While the authors and publishers regret any inconvenience this may cause the readers, no responsibility for any such changes can be accepted by either the authors or the publisher.

Cover photograph: NASA

Photo credits: p. 5: Chris Fairclough/cfwimages.com; p. 6: Discovery Books; p. 8: NASA/JPL-Caltech/S. Wilner; p. 9: Andrea Leone/istockphoto.com; p. 10: Robert & Linda Mostyn; Eye Ubiquitous/Corbis; p. 11: Kean Collection/Getty Images; p. 13: Eliza Snow/istockphoto.com; p. 14: Kiyoshi Takahase/istockphoto.com; p. 15: Sheila Terry/Science Photo Library; p. 16: Gary Allard/istockphoto.com; p. 18: Corbis; p. 21: Edward Parker/EASI-Images/cfwimages.com; p. 24: Hulton Archive/Getty images; p. 25: ESA; p. 26: Warren Gretz/NREL; p. 30: ETH Zurich/Pac-Car II; p. 33: Edward Parker/EASI-Images/cfwimages.com; p. 34: Roger Whiteway/istockphoto.com; p. 35: Rob Bowden/EASI-Images/cfwimages.com; p. 36: The Brown Reference Group; p. 37: Imagno/Getty Images; p. 40: NASA/MODIS Land Rapid Response Team, Jeff Schmaltz; p. 42: Don F. Figer (UCLA)/NASA; p. 43: NASA; p. 44: Nebraska Soybean Board/NREL

Contents

CHAPTER I

What is energy?

What would a world without energy be like? If there was a power cut to your house, the lights would not work, the TV would be blank, and if you used an electric cooker you would not be able to cook. If your car ran out of fuel, the engine would have no energy to make it work, and the car would not move. Without energy from food animals cannot survive, and without energy from sunlight plants cannot grow. A world without energy would be cold, dark, still and lifeless.

So what *is* energy?

We have seen that without energy, nothing happens. So one way of describing energy is to say that it is the ability to make things happen. When electrical energy flows through the wiring in a house, the lights work, the television comes on and the cooker heats up. If the car has a full tank of fuel, you can travel for many miles without stopping. Animals that have eaten have the energy to survive and look for more food. Plants that get regular sunlight grow and produce flowers and fruit.

 AMAZING FACTS

World's biggest power cut

The power cut that probably affected more people than any other happened on 14 August 2003. A problem with a power company in Canada caused a blackout across the eastern USA and Canada, affecting more than 50 million people. Traffic lights failed, underground railways stopped, and people were trapped in lifts. In New York City millions of people had to walk home, and some who lived too far away ended up sleeping on the streets for the night.

Another way of describing energy is that it is the capacity to do work. 'Work' can mean all kinds of things, from switching on a light bulb to growing a flower. This definition of energy is not much different from the first one, but as we will see later in the book, it is helpful when we want to measure energy.

A world of energy

In this book we will look at different types of energy. We will look at how energy can move from place to place, and how it changes from one form to another. We will see how living things depend on the Sun's energy. Energy cannot be created or destroyed – so why are people worried that our energy might run out? There is always the same amount of energy before and after it changes form, so why do we talk about wasting energy? Read on to find the answers.

A large city uses an enormous amount of energy just to keep the streets and buildings lit at night.

CHAPTER 2

Adaptable energy

Energy comes in a bewildering variety of forms. Light and heat are both forms of energy, and sound is energy, too. Electricity is a very versatile kind of energy – we use it for all kinds of purposes. Anything that is moving has energy, including things like the wind (moving air) and waves (moving water). The energy of movement is called kinetic energy.

Potential energy

Things do not have to be hot, or moving, or making a noise to have energy. They could have potential energy. This is the energy that is not actually making something happen right now, but it could do at any moment. For instance, a person on a high diving board could be perfectly still and quiet, but they have the potential to dive or jump into the water below.

In a few seconds, this diver will be rushing downwards towards the pool with a large amount of kinetic energy.

Water held in a **reservoir** by a dam also has potential energy. The water in the reservoir is still and quiet. But if we open the **sluice gates**, water rushes down tunnels and pipes until it reaches a water turbine (see page 25). By this time it has enough kinetic energy to be able to turn the water turbine.

The potential energy of a diver or the water in a reservoir comes from gravity. The diver is supported against the pull of gravity by the diving board, while the water is held back by the dam. When the diver goes off the board, or the sluice gates open, gravity is free to act and the diver (or water) begins to fall.

Chemical energy

Another kind of energy is the energy that a car gets from its fuel, or that we can get from a fire. These types of energy come from burning, which is a chemical reaction. The energy that we get from our food is also a chemical reaction. These kinds of energy are known as chemical energy. Chemical energy is stored in a fuel or other chemical, ready to be converted into heat, light or some other form of energy.

 HIGH-OCTANE FUEL

Petrol and diesel are good fuels because they contain more energy per litre than other fuels, as this table shows.

Fuel type	Energy megajoules (million **joules**) per litre
Diesel	40.9
Petrol	32.0
LPG (liquified petroleum gas)	22.16
Ethanol (alcohol)	19.59
Methanol	14.57

Energy transfer

Moving energy from one place to another, or from one object to another, is known as an energy transfer. Sometimes energy transfers are very useful to us, but at other times we want to stop them from happening.

One of the most useful things about electricity is that it is a form of energy that we can easily move. Overhead and underground cables carry electricity from power stations to homes, shops, offices and factories over a large area, while smaller wires carry electricity to different parts of a house or other building.

Sound is another kind of energy that can travel. When we talk to each other, for instance, we are transferring sound energy from one place to another. A lion's roar or an elephant's low rumble can be heard for several kilometres, and the 'songs' of some whales can travel hundreds of kilometres through the water.

 ## AMAZING FACTS

Well-travelled light

Two galaxies discovered in 2004 are the most distant that we know of. Both galaxies are 13 billion light years or more from the Earth. This means that the light energy from these galaxies has taken 13 billion years to reach us. In one year, light travels 9.5 trillion (9,500,000,000,000) kilometres, or 5.9 trillion miles, so light from these galaxies has travelled 123.5 billion trillion kilometres, or 76.7 billion trillion miles.

The galaxy in this photograph, Messier 81, is 12 million light years away.

The best way of moving energy over really long distances is as light or some other form of **electromagnetic radiation** (such as radio waves, microwaves or X-rays). Light from the Sun travels about 150 million kilometres (93 million miles) to pour energy onto the Earth. Without this energy we would not be able to see, and plants would not be able to make their own food. Heat from the Sun is also a type of electromagnetic radiation. Heat can also be transferred from one place to another in other ways (see pages 18/19).

Kinetic energy is movement energy, so it obviously moves from place to place. But kinetic energy can also be transferred from one object to another. For instance, when you kick a football you transfer kinetic energy from your foot to the ball, while in cricket and tennis you transfer energy to the ball from a bat or racket.

In baseball, the energy from the batter's swing is transferred from the bat to the ball.

Transforming energy

When a diver jumps from a diving board, or the **sluice gates** are opened on a dam, the potential energy of the diver or the **reservoir** is changed into another kind of energy – kinetic energy. Energy transformations are central to the many ways that we make use of energy. Electrical energy, for example, has to be transformed into some other kind of energy in order for us to use it. Light bulbs turn electrical energy into light, electric fires and cookers turn electrical energy into heat, motors turn electricity into movement and loudspeakers turn it into sound. Other devices work the other way, turning some other kind of energy into electrical energy. A microphone, for example, turns sounds into electrical signals.

Many machines involve more than one energy transformation. For instance in a car, chemical energy (the fuel) is converted in the engine into heat (the fuel burns). The heat is then used to drive the engine and make the car move, so the heat energy is converted into kinetic energy.

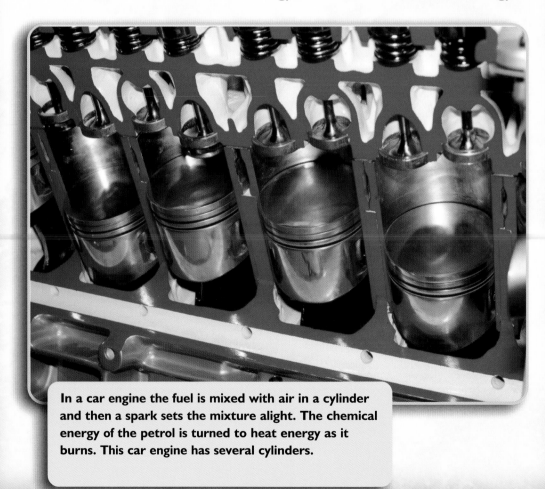

In a car engine the fuel is mixed with air in a cylinder and then a spark sets the mixture alight. The chemical energy of the petrol is turned to heat energy as it burns. This car engine has several cylinders.

A swinging converter

One of the most interesting energy converters is a pendulum. Pendulums are sometimes used in clocks, because the speed of their swing stays constant.

As a pendulum swings from side to side it is constantly transforming energy. At the top of its swing, a pendulum is still. At that moment it has no kinetic energy. However, it has maximum potential energy because it is at the highest point in its swing. As the pendulum swings down it gradually gathers speed, until at the bottom of its swing it is moving its fastest. At this point the pendulum has maximum kinetic energy but no potential energy. In each swing, the pendulum converts potential energy to kinetic energy and back again.

GREAT SCIENTISTS

Galileo's pendulum

The great Italian scientist Galileo Galilei (1564-1642) first noticed that a pendulum had a constant time for each swing while watching a chandelier in a cathedral. He carried out a series of experiments to show that a pendulum takes the same amount of time for each swing. He began to use pendulums as clocks, timing events by the number of swings of a pendulum. Although he did not build a working clock, Galileo did begin work on one. The first working pendulum clock was actually built in 1657, by the Dutch scientist Christaan Huygens.

A portrait of Galileo Galilei. Although Galileo never finished building a clock, he did design one. His son built the clock after Galileo's death.

Measuring energy

One of the definitions of energy at the start of the book was that it is 'the capacity to do work'. The advantage of this way of thinking about energy is that we can use a pre-existing scientific definition of work. This means that work, and therefore energy, can be measured. Work is the force needed to move an object multiplied by the distance it moves:

$$work = force \times distance$$

The work done (the energy involved) is measured in units called **joules (J)**. One joule is the work done when a force of 1 **newton** (N) is moved 1 metre.

 GREAT EXPERIMENTS

James Joule

The unit of energy is named after the English scientist James Joule (1818-1889). Joule showed that mechanical work (for instance turning a wheel or moving a weight) can be converted directly into heat. For years, scientists were not convinced, so Joule designed many experiments to demonstrate that he was correct. His most effective experiment was one in which he placed paddle wheels in an **insulated** barrel full of water, and made them turn by attaching them to a falling weight. By careful measurement of the temperature before and after the experiment, he showed that the mechanical work of turning the paddles had heated up the water.

Sometimes energy is measured in other units. For instance, people often talk about the number of calories in the food they eat, and calories (cal) are a measure of energy. One calorie is equal to about 4.2 joules. An average girl aged 11 to 14 needs to eat about 1,850 **kilocalories** (kcal) or 7,745 **kilojoules** (kJ) of food a day to keep healthy, while a boy needs slightly more – 2,220 kcal, or 9,259 kJ, per day.

Athletes use large amounts of energy during training and in races. A top athlete may need to eat 4,000-5,000 kcal (16,740-20,930 kJ) or more per day in order to stay healthy.

Energy and power

In ordinary speech people often use the words 'energy' and 'power' almost interchangeably, but in science the words have different meanings. If energy is the amount of work needed to do a task, power is the amount of energy used in a certain amount of time to do the task. If energy is measured in joules and time is measured in seconds, the unit of power is **watts (W)**. For instance, if you use a force of 10 newtons to move an object 10 metres, it will take 100 joules of energy. If you move the object in 10 seconds, this means you are using a power of 10 watts (10 joules per second). If, however, you move the object in 1 second you use 100 watts of power.

 ## WATTS AND LIGHT BULBS

The power of the light bulbs in your house is usually measured in watts. The most common bulbs are 40, 60 and 100 watts. A 100-watt bulb uses 100 joules of electrical energy every second. Energy-saving bulbs cost more than 'normal' bulbs, but they use less power. A 20W energy-saving bulb is brighter than a 100W normal bulb, but it uses a fifth of the energy.

CHAPTER 3

Heat energy

Many scientists thought that heat was a substance until well into the nineteenth century. Today we know that heat is a form of energy. Energy is the ability to do work, and heat does lots of work for us. Heat cooks food for us and warms our homes. Heat makes car engines work and most power stations use heat to produce electricity. Warm-blooded animals such as mammals and birds generate heat in their bodies so that they can stay active in cold weather.

Heat is a form of kinetic energy, because it is produced by movement. How hot a substance is relates to the amount of movement in the tiny particles (**atoms** and **molecules**) that make up all substances.

Warm-blooded animals must use extra energy to keep their bodies warm. This is particularly difficult for small animals like this hummingbird. They must eat constantly to survive.

 GREAT SCIENTISTS

Antoine Lavoisier

In his book *The Elements of Chemistry* (1787), the French chemist Antoine Lavoisier listed 32 substances that he considered to be elements (substances that could not be broken down further into simpler substances). One of these 'elements' was a substance that he called caloric. We know it better as heat. It took another century to prove that heat was not a substance, but a form of energy instead.

Rumford's boring barrels

The person who first began to understand the nature of heat was Benjamin Thompson (later Count Rumford). In the 1790s Thompson was supervising work in a factory making cannons. He observed that when the insides of the cannon were being bored (smoothed by turning a special tool inside the barrel), a great deal of heat was generated. He carried out a series of experiments to measure the heat produced by the boring process.

Rumford thought that his experiments proved that the heat was being generated by the motion of the boring tool in the cannon barrel (today we would say that the heat was the result of **friction** between the barrel and the boring tool). However other scientists of the time were not convinced. The idea of heat as a substance persisted until Joule proved the connection between work and heat in the mid-nineteenth century (see page 12).

This illustration shows Rumford demonstrating how heat is created when boring a cannon.

The particles in a solid do not have much space to move. They vibrate back and forth about a central point. As the temperature of a solid rises, these vibrations get bigger and bigger until the solid melts and becomes liquid. In a liquid, particles have more freedom to move, and heating makes the particles move faster until the liquid turns into a gas. In a gas, the particles can move in any direction. The particles in a hot gas move faster than those in a cold gas.

Heat and temperature

Heat and temperature are not the same thing. The amount of heat in an object is the total heat energy of all the particles in the object. The temperature, on the other hand, is a measure of the average energy of the particles. There are plenty of examples of this all around us. The glowing **filament** in a light bulb has a high temperature, but it does not have much total heat. A bath full of hot water is at a much lower temperature, but it contains far more total heat.

Heat flow

If you get a phone call just as you finish making a cup of hot chocolate, you might forget about your drink. When you remember it an hour later, the chocolate will no longer be hot. This is an example of a general rule about heat – heat flows from areas of high temperature to areas of low temperature. The hot chocolate was originally at a higher temperature than its surroundings, but gradually it cools as heat flows from the hot drink into the surroundings.

Although the hot chocolate is hotter than its surroundings, it has far less heat overall than the surroundings. The heat energy from the hot chocolate is not enough to make the room significantly warmer. If you put a hot water bottle in your bed, the situation is different. Heat flows from the hot water bottle, which is at a higher temperature, to the bedclothes, which are at a lower temperature. However, there is more heat energy in the hot water bottle, and a bed is a smaller space than a room. As the hot water bottle cools down, the temperature of the bed gets higher. Eventually the hot water bottle and the bed reach the same temperature, and the flow of heat stops.

A mug of hot tea will eventually become cold as the heat from the mug flows to the room, however the total heat of the mug is not enough to warm the room around it.

AMAZING FACTS

Highs and lows

There is no upper limit to the temperature a substance can reach. The surface of the Sun has a temperature of about 9900 °F (5500 °C), but the core (centre) has a temperature of 15-16 million °C (59-61 million °F). Other stars are considerably hotter than the Sun, and other objects in space have even higher temperatures. However, there is a lower limit to temperature. **Absolute zero** is the lowest temperature that a substance can reach, when the movement of its particles is at the absolute minimum. The temperature of absolute zero is -273.16 °C, or -459.67 °F.

15-16 million °C
core of Sun

5500 °C
surface of Sun

2500 °C light bulb filament

2000 °C gas flame

1535 °C iron melts

100 °C water boils

37 °C human body

0 °C water freezes

-18 °C frozen food

-200 °C liquid oxygen

-273.16 °C absolute zero

The temperature scale ranges from absolute zero to millions of degrees.

Types of heat flow

Heat flows from place to place in several different ways. Think first about a spoon in a cup of hot chocolate. At first, the handle sticking out of the drink is cool, but after a few minutes it is as hot as the rest of the spoon. Heat has flowed along the spoon by a process called conduction. Hot particles in one part of the solid pass on some of their heat energy to the particles close to them. These particles pass on energy to the particles close to them, and so on.

Conductors and insulators

Not all materials conduct heat in the same way. A plastic spoon standing in a hot drink takes far longer to heat up than a metal one. Most metals are good conductors of heat. This makes metals good for the bodies of saucepans, but not so good for the handles. Instead, plastic, rubber and wood are examples of poor heat conductors, or insulators.

Polar bears have such good insulation that they sometimes get too hot! As well as their thick fur, they have an **insulating** layer of blubber (fat), which keeps them warm in the water as well as on land.

Convection

When we heat a pan of water, heat spreads through the water by a different process, known as **convection**. The water at the base of the pan is heated first. Warm water is less dense (or lighter) than cold water, so the heated water rises. Colder water then flows in to replace it. The result is a current, known as a convection current, in which the warmer water at the bottom of the pan is constantly being replaced by colder water from above. Something similar happens when any fluid (liquid or gas) is heated.

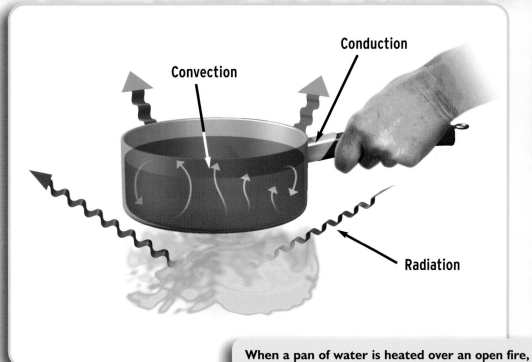

Conduction

Convection

Radiation

When a pan of water is heated over an open fire, all three kinds of heat transfer happen at the same time. Heat is conducted from the body of the pan along the handle. Convection carries heat around the water in the pan. Finally, heat radiates from the fire.

Radiation

Heat cannot travel through space by conduction or convection. Heat from the Sun reaches us by a third process, known as radiation. Heat radiation is a kind of **electromagnetic radiation** (see page 9), known as **infra-red** radiation. Like light, infra-red radiation travels incredibly quickly – it takes just 8 minutes for heat from the Sun to reach the Earth. Many hot objects on Earth, such as the hotplates on a cooker, also radiate heat.

 HEAT FROM THE STARS

Distant stars and galaxies produce infra-red radiation just like the Sun, but it is hard to detect from Earth. The Spitzer Space Telescope solves this problem by being positioned far out in space. The telescope is shielded from the heat of the Sun, and its instruments are cooled to almost **absolute zero**. This enables it to pick up very faint infra-red signals from space.

CHAPTER 4

Energy resources

In the modern world we use energy for almost everything we do. Most of this energy comes from what we call energy resources. Between getting up in the morning and arriving at school, you probably use all kinds of energy resources. If you have a shower in the morning, the water is probably heated by electrical energy. If it is a cold day, the heating will be on. The heat energy could come from oil, gas, coal, wood or electricity. Any lights you switch on will use electricity, as will the radio or TV. If you go to school in a car or a bus, it will need energy from petrol or diesel fuel. Electricity, oil, fuel, gas, coal and wood are just some of the energy resources that we rely on every day.

The pie chart shows world electricity production in 2003. Over 85 per cent of the world's electricity was produced using coal, oil or natural gas.

World fuel consumption

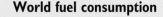

- Coal – 23.9%
- Natural gas – 26.3%
- Crude oil – 35.4%
- Nuclear power – 6.4%
- Hydroelectric power – 6.6%
- Geothermal and other – 1.4%

 ## MEASURING THE ENERGY IN FUELS

The best way to find out how much energy there is in a particular fuel is to burn some. However, it is difficult to measure energy directly from burning. Instead, scientists burn a measured amount of fuel under carefully controlled conditions, and use it to heat water. By measuring the temperature of the water before and after burning the fuel, and knowing the volume of the water, it is possible to work out how much heat energy the fuel produced.

Energy from fuels

Oil, gas, wood, petrol and diesel are all different types of fuel. We have seen already that fuels are a type of chemical energy and that we get energy from fuels by combustion (burning). Combustion is a chemical reaction that releases heat energy. We can use this heat directly, for instance, to heat a house or other building. We can also use the heat to generate another kind of energy. In a car or other vehicle, the heat energy is converted into kinetic energy (movement). The other major way we use fuels is to generate electricity.

Electricity from fuels

Electricity is a very convenient kind of energy. It is also a clean form of energy – when things run on electricity, no smoke or fumes are created. This is why we use it in so many ways. However, electricity has to be generated somehow. The main way this is done is by burning some kind of fuel, usually oil, coal or natural gas. The fuel is burned in a furnace, which heats water to make steam. The steam is pushed at high pressure through a machine called a steam turbine, which spins at high speed. The steam turbine is used to turn a generator, which produces electricity.

Cooling towers pour out steam and fumes from a coal-burning power station.

Fossil fuels

Coal, oil and natural gas are collectively known as fossil fuels. This is because these materials were formed from the remains of plants and animals that lived hundreds of millions of years ago. Fossil fuels took millions of years to form. Although large amounts are found in underground rocks and occasionally at the surface, supplies of fossil fuels are limited. What is more, once they have been used up, these fuels cannot be replaced. This situation is worrying because we rely so heavily on fossil fuels for energy.

How fossil fuels formed

Most of our coal deposits formed during the Carboniferous period. This was between 290 and 354 million years ago, at least 40 million years before dinosaurs existed. During the Carboniferous period large parts of the Earth were covered by vast, swampy forests. The trees and other plants in these forests rotted very slowly after they died. Over thousands of years they formed a layer of spongy material called peat. Gradually the peat became buried under other rocks, which squashed down the peat layer. After years under pressure, the soft peat hardened into coal.

As with coal deposits, most of our oil and gas supplies formed over 300 million years ago. However, oil and gas formed in the sea rather than in forests. The seas swarmed with microscopic plants and animals known as plankton. When the plankton died, they fell to the sea bed. A layer of plankton, mixed with mud, slowly built up over the years. Later these remains were buried, squashed and also heated. The combination of pressure and heating slowly turned the mixture into oil or gas, depending on the temperature (gas formed at higher temperatures than oil).

 AMAZING FACTS

Prehistoric gas

Research carried out in 2003 showed that about 23.5 tonnes of ancient plant and animal material goes to make one litre of oil. So to fill the 60-litre tank of a typical family car takes the equivalent of 1,410 tonnes of prehistoric plants.

The oil and gas were lighter than the surrounding rocks, so slowly they filtered upwards through the rocks above them. In some places the oil or gas reached the surface. In other places the oil or gas became trapped under a layer of **impermeable** rock that they could not filter through. This is how the oil and gas deposits we find today were formed.

COAL, OIL AND GAS

How oil and gas were formed (top right-hand steps). 1) Oil and gas begin as tiny sea creatures that swarm in the waters. 2) As they die, they sink to the seabed. 3) The layer of dead sea creatures is buried. As it is buried deeper and gets hot, the layer turns to oil and gas. 4) Oil and gas slowly rise up through the tiny pores in the rock. 5) A layer of dense rock does not let oil and gas pass through and it becomes trapped.

How coal was formed (lower left-hand steps). 6) About 1,300 million years ago, large areas of swampy forest covered the Earth. 7) As the trees died, they were buried under a layer of mud and sand. 8) As more material built up above, the layer of rotted plant material was squashed. 9) Further pressure and heat in the earth turned the plant material into coal.

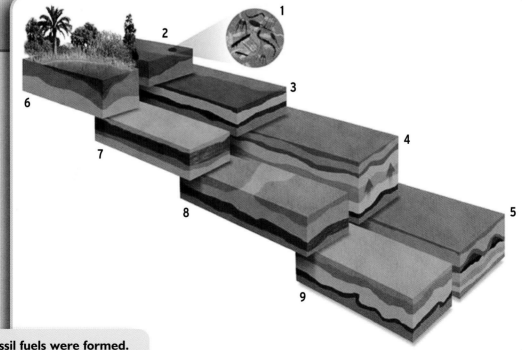

How fossil fuels were formed.

Fossil fuel alternatives

We produce so much energy using fossil fuels that they will be hard to replace. However, there are good reasons to look for alternative energy resources. As we have seen, fossil fuels are not renewable and will eventually run out. Another problem is that burning fossil fuels releases polluting gases. Burning fossil fuels also produces large amounts of carbon dioxide, a gas which is a major cause of **global warming**.

Nuclear power

Nuclear power is the most widely used form of energy after fossil fuels. As in a fossil fuel power station, a nuclear power station produces heat to make steam, which powers a steam turbine. However, the heat is produced in a nuclear reaction, in which **atoms** of the **radioactive** metal uranium are split in two, with the release of large amounts of energy. This is called a nuclear reaction because it involves the nucleus (central part) of the atom. Nuclear power stations produce large amounts of energy using only small amounts of fuel. However, they are expensive to build, and an accident can cause the release of large amounts of radioactivity.

AMAZING FACTS

The first nuclear reactor

In 1942, the Italian physicist Enrico Fermi directed the building of the first ever nuclear reactor, in an old sports hall at Chicago University. The reactor was called a 'nuclear pile', because it was literally a carefully stacked pile of carbon blocks and small pellets of uranium.

A photograph of Enrico Fermi (1901-1954), taken around the time he built his 'nuclear pile'.

Hydroelectric power

Hydroelectric power is another form of energy that is widely used. The energy to turn the electric generators comes from water held back behind a large dam. Where there are suitable rivers, hydroelectric power can produce cheap electricity without pollution. However, dams can flood large areas of productive land, and they can have a bad effect on agriculture and fishing downstream of the dam.

The Three Gorges Dam on the Yangtze River in China is the largest ever hydroelectric project. At full power the dam will produce 18 billion **watts** of power. Over a million people have had to move from their homes to make space for the **reservoir**.

Wind power

Windmills have been used for thousands of years to pump water and grind cereals into flour. Today, propeller-style wind generators are increasingly used to produce electricity. They are most effective in windy locations such as high ground, coastal areas and offshore.

Single wind generators do not produce large amounts of power, so they are often grouped together in 'wind farms'. Over the long term wind is a reliable source of energy, but there are large variations in the amount of wind day by day. Wind farms can also be noisy, and many people dislike the look of them.

Biomass and biofuels

Biomass is any material that comes from living things. At its simplest, biomass energy is a power station using wood instead of fossil fuels. Plant and animal materials other than wood are not good fuels when used directly. However, crops such as corn and sugar beet can be turned into useful fuels such as ethanol (alcohol) and biodiesel. Also, a wide range of biomass materials, including agricultural waste and animal dung, can be converted into gas. This is done either by **fermenting** with **bacteria** or by heating under special conditions. Biomass and biofuels are often used for CHP (combined heat and power) generation. In a CHP power plant, 'waste' heat produced while generating electricity is used to heat local buildings.

This power station in Burlington, Vermont, USA, is a biomass gasifier. Here wood chips are turned into electricity.

Solar power

The Sun is an inexhaustible energy source that is available every day. However, hardly any power stations have been built to use solar power because no cheap, effective way has been found to harness the Sun's power on a large scale. However, many homeowners have solar cells, which convert sunlight directly into electricity, on the roof of their house. Solar cells are also used to power a wide range of electrical devices, from calculators to the International Space Station.

Other energy resources

Other energy resources that are used in a limited way for power generation are the power of the waves and tides, and geothermal energy (heat energy from underground). Deep below the Earth's surface the rocks are so hot that they are almost molten, and in a few places, cracks and holes in the Earth's crust allow these hot rocks close to the surface, where they can be used as a source of power.

Geothermal energy is an excellent source of power in places such as Iceland, Japan and New Zealand, where there is an area of hot rocks fairly close to the surface. However, there are very few good sites for geothermal power.

Early tidal power stations involved building a long barrage or barrier across a river or estuary, and used the power of the tide to drive turbines in the barrier. This kind of power station was expensive to build, and there were only a few suitable sites. More recent tidal power designs are cheaper and can be built in many more places, but as yet the ideas are untested. Similarly, there has been much work on developing practical ideas for wave-powered generators, but as yet no large wave-powered power stations exist.

 COMPARING FUEL RESOURCES

Resource	Advantages	Disadvantages	Renewable?
Fossil fuels	• Generate lots of power cheaply • Easy to transport • Modern power stations efficient	• Produce pollution • Produce carbon dioxide • Coal mining difficult and dangerous • Mining damages landscape	No
Nuclear power	• Costs about same as fossil fuels • High energy from a small amount • No air pollution • No carbon dioxide emissions	• Waste very dangerous • High costs to ensure safety • An accident can release huge amounts of **radioactivity**	No
Hydroelectricity	• Energy almost free once dam built • Reliable, constant energy source • No waste or pollution • Dam can be used for irrigating crops	• Dams expensive to build • Causes flooding upstream • Can affect wildlife and agriculture downstream	Yes
Wind power	• Free once generators built • No pollution or waste • Land nearby can be farmed • Good for remote areas	• Intermittent source of energy • Low energy output • Only suitable for some locations • Can be noisy	Yes
Biomass	• Fuels usually cheap • Can use up waste materials • Does not increase carbon dioxide	• Can be difficult to get enough • Burning produces carbon dioxide and some pollutants	Yes
Solar power	• Free source of energy • Good for remote locations or warm countries • Can be used on small scale	• Power stations expensive • Does not work at night • Unreliable except in sunny places	Yes

CHAPTER 5

Energy savings and efficiency

Imagine you are cycling down a long, flat road. As you cycle along you are turning chemical energy from your muscles into kinetic energy (movement of the bike). At some point you decide to stop pedalling. The bike slows down, and soon you stop. What happened to all that energy you put into the bike? It seems to have disappeared. But as we will see, the energy has just changed into another form.

Friction and air resistance

When you cycle along an open road, it seems that there is nothing to hold you back. However, there is a force trying to stop you all the time. This force is **friction**. Friction between the road and the bike tyres gives you grip and stops the bike from slipping. However, this friction also slows you down. There is friction in the wheel bearings, too, even though they are greased to make them move freely.

As you cycle along you feel a wind on your face, even though there is no wind when you stop. The wind is produced by another kind of friction called air resistance. If you wade through water, you can feel how the water resists your progress. Air is thinner than water, but it still offers some resistance as you move through it, and you feel this resistance as wind.

 DANGEROUS BRAKES

Most bikes have rubber or plastic brake blocks that press against the wheel rim to slow down or stop. This design has the disadvantage that the rims get hot through friction with the brake pads. On a heavily loaded bike in a hilly area, constant braking can heat the rims so much that the inner tube on the tyre expands, and sometimes bursts.

No energy lost

Friction and air resistance are the main forces that slow the bike down when you stop pedalling. As they act, the bike loses its kinetic energy. However, the energy does not just disappear. Most of the kinetic energy transforms into heat, as the bearings, the bicycle tyres and the road are all warmed up by friction. A small amount of energy transforms into sound – the rumbling sound of the tyres on the road. None of the energy is actually lost. In fact, it is a general law of physics that energy is never made or destroyed. This is known as the law of conservation of energy.

How a cyclist on a flat road loses energy. If the rider is cycling into a headwind, the air resistance will be greater, and they will lose energy more quickly.

drag
(air resistance)

22 km/hr

friction
(rolling resistance)

'Wasted' energy

If you had a bike with rusty wheel bearings it would be much harder to pedal, and the bike would slow down more quickly when you stopped pedalling. Much of the energy you used for pedalling would be lost. It would go towards heating up the bearings rather than moving the bike along.

In any kind of process only some of the energy is converted into useful work. The rest of the energy is 'wasted', often becoming heat energy. The percentage of energy that is converted into useful work is known as the efficiency of the process. A bicycle is very efficient. Up to 99 per cent of the energy you use pressing down on the pedals is converted into movement of the bike on the road.

 AMAZING FACTS

Less power than a light bulb

Probably the world's most fuel-efficient vehicle is a car built by a team of designers at the Federal Institute of Technology in Zurich, Switzerland. In 2005 their hydrogen-powered vehicle managed a fuel consumption of 5,835 kilometres per litre of fuel – or 16,486 miles per gallon. The power needed to keep it going is less than that of most conventional light bulbs.

In 2005 PAC-Car II set a fuel efficiency record of 16,486 miles per gallon. The car was powered by electricity, produced by a hydrogen fuel cell.

Improving efficiency

No other machines are as efficient as bicycles. Machines that have an engine of some kind – everything from lawnmowers to rockets – have a maximum energy efficiency of around 68 per cent. This is to do with the nature of engines. They must produce some heat, or they don't work, and that heat is 'waste' energy.

Most conventional power stations have a much lower efficiency than 68 per cent. An average fossil fuel power station has an efficiency of around 35 per cent, although more recent gas-powered stations can be up to 60 per cent efficient. Most efficient of all are CHP (combined heat and power) power stations. Because they use the 'waste' heat as well as producing electricity, the efficiency of a CHP plant can reach 70-80 per cent.

Some methods of power generation do not involve using engines. Large **hydroelectric power** plants have efficiencies of between 70 and 90 per cent. Wind turbines can reach efficiencies of 60 per cent, while solar panels have an efficiency of only 8-15 per cent. However, in these kinds of technology, where the energy is 'free', efficiency is less important than the cost of producing the electricity.

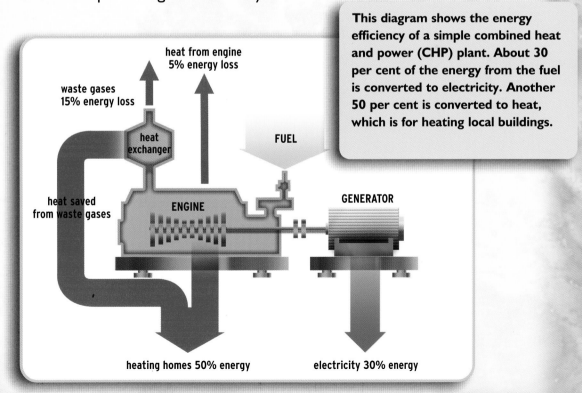

This diagram shows the energy efficiency of a simple combined heat and power (CHP) plant. About 30 per cent of the energy from the fuel is converted to electricity. Another 50 per cent is converted to heat, which is for heating local buildings.

heat from engine
5% energy loss

waste gases
15% energy loss

heat
exchanger

FUEL

heat saved
from waste gases

ENGINE

GENERATOR

heating homes 50% energy

electricity 30% energy

CHAPTER 6

Living energy

The energy you need to pedal a bike comes from your muscles, but where do your muscles get their energy from? The energy to power muscles comes from food. This can be either from eating meat or plants. Plants themselves do not eat food – they make their own using energy from sunlight.

Energy for plants

Plants make food from light through the process of photosynthesis. In photosynthesis, light energy from the Sun is converted into the chemical energy of foods such as sugars.

Photosynthesis happens in a plant's leaves. The first stage involves light. Light is absorbed by coloured pigments in the plant's leaves, in particular a green pigment called chlorophyll. The light energy gained is used to make a substance called ATP (adenosine triphosphate). ATP is the main energy carrier in living things – it is like energy 'money'.

 GREAT EXPERIMENTS

Priestley and photosynthesis

The main 'waste product' of photosynthesis is oxygen. Oxygen is essential for things to burn, and animals need it to breathe. The English chemist Joseph Priestley showed in a series of experiments that plants produce oxygen. In one experiment he put a sprig of mint in a sealed glass jar with a candle. He then lit the candle (by focusing sunlight on the wick). The candle went out when there was no oxygen left in the jar. Priestley then left the sealed jar for 27 days. At the end of this time he lit the candle once more, and it was able to burn. Through this experiment he showed that plants produce oxygen. Soon afterwards, in 1779, the Dutch-born scientist Jan Ingenhousz showed that plants need light in order to produce oxygen.

The second stage in photosynthesis does not need light. In this stage, carbon dioxide from the air is combined with water from the soil to make sugars. The sugars act as food for other parts of the plant. The energy needed to power this process comes from the ATP 'money' made in the first stage of photosynthesis.

Energy efficiency

The efficiency of photosynthesis is very low. If you measure how much light falls on a particular area of soil in one year, then measure the weight of plants that can be grown on that area in a year, this gives an idea of the efficiency of photosynthesis. This can vary, depending on the plant, from less than 1 per cent to about 3.5 per cent.

A few plants, such as sugar cane, are very efficient at photosynthesis. They can turn up to 3.5 per cent of the Sun's energy into plant material.

Food energy

Animals cannot turn sunlight into food as plants do. They have to eat some kind of food to get energy. No animals can feed on inorganic materials, such as rocks or air. Their food has to come from plants or from other animals.

Plant eaters

Animals that eat plants are called herbivores. They have a plentiful supply of food, but it can be difficult for them to get useful energy from it. This is because plants have large amounts of energy locked up in materials such as cellulose (a stringy material found in most plants) and lignin (a tough substance found in large amounts in trees and other woody plants). Many plant eaters have found ways to digest and use the energy from cellulose. However, only a few animals (for instance termites) are able to digest wood.

On average, only about 10 per cent of the plant material that herbivores eat is turned into **animal tissue**. The rest is used up in activities such as looking for food or finding a mate, or is lost as heat. So it takes 400 kg of grass to keep a 4-kg rabbit alive.

Herbivores, such as these fallow deer, must constantly graze on plants to keep healthy.

COMPLETING THE CYCLE

Plants and animals do not have to be living to provide a source of food. A whole range of living things, from beetles to **bacteria**, feed on dead and rotting things and on animal waste. These decomposers, as they are known, eventually reduce all animal and plant tissue to a few simple chemicals which enrich the soil.

Animal eaters

Animals that eat other animals are known as carnivores. It is easier for carnivores to digest their food and turn it into energy, but their food is harder to obtain – they have to hunt for it. As with herbivores, carnivores convert about 10 per cent of herbivore tissue, on average, into body tissue.

Some animals are much less efficient at converting food into body weight than others. Mammals and birds, for instance, convert only about 2 per cent of their food into body weight. This is because they use a large part of their energy to keep their bodies at a constant temperature. However, animals such as reptiles and amphibians, which do not use food energy to keep their bodies warm, can convert up to 20 per cent of their food into body weight.

Studies in the Serengeti plains of Africa have shown that one lion needs a population of 350 grazing animals to feed on.

CHAPTER 7

Keeping the Earth going

A volcano can pour out hot lava, ash and dust for days on end. An earthquake can destroy houses for miles around its centre. An ocean storm can toss a huge tanker like a toy. Natural events like these show that the Earth can produce enormous amounts of energy. Where does this energy come from?

Energy beneath the Earth

The rocks beneath our feet form only a thin crust over the Earth's surface. If the Earth were the size of an apple, the crust would be about as thick as the apple's skin. Below the crust is a layer of very hot, partly molten rock known as the mantle. Below this is a third layer called the core, which has a fluid outer part and is solid at the centre.

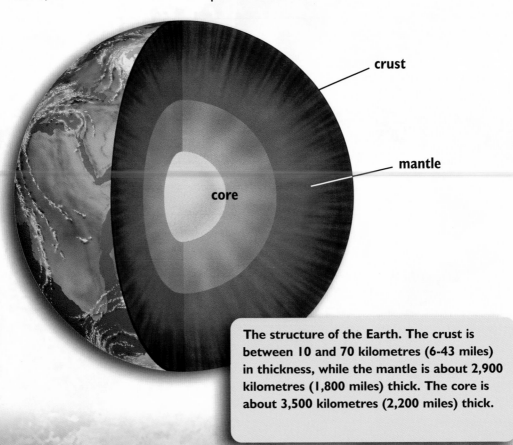

crust

mantle

core

The structure of the Earth. The crust is between 10 and 70 kilometres (6-43 miles) in thickness, while the mantle is about 2,900 kilometres (1,800 miles) thick. The core is about 3,500 kilometres (2,200 miles) thick.

The mantle is heated by **radioactive** (nuclear) reactions going on within it. Rocks that are closer to the surface are cooler than those below. The hotter rocks are less dense, and they slowly rise up through the mantle. At the same time, cooler rocks sink down deeper into the mantle. The result is huge **convection** currents, similar to those in a pan of heated water. However, these convection currents move very slowly, because the mantle rocks are like thick molasses rather than water. It takes millions of years for rock to circulate through the mantle.

Movements on the surface

The convection movements of the mantle cause movements in the Earth's crust. The crust is cracked and broken into a number of large pieces known as plates. These plates move along with the mantle beneath them. Plates may move towards each other, or apart, or side by side in opposite directions. Earthquakes are caused when two plates suddenly shift against each other. Volcanoes happen where hot rocks seep upwards through cracks and gaps in colliding plates.

GREAT SCIENTISTS

Alfred Wegener

The German scientist Alfred Wegener (1880-1930) first put forward the theory that the Earth's crust is broken into moving plates. Wegener read research showing that similar fossils had been found on widely separated continents, and he noticed that the coasts of south America and Africa could fit together. He suggested that the continents had at one time been joined in one giant land mass. Wegener gathered much evidence to support his theory, but other scientists were not convinced. Plate tectonics, as his theory is called, was not fully accepted until the 1960s.

A photograph of geophysicist and meteorologist Alfred Wegener, taken around 1920.

Energy from the Sun

Apart from movement of the Earth's plates, most events on the Earth's surface are fuelled by energy from the Sun.

About 400 million billion **joules** of energy reach us from the Sun every second. That's 32 million times more energy than the world's largest power station can produce. This energy does not fall evenly all over the Earth. Because the world is spherical, and it is tilted on its axis, some parts of the Earth receive far more energy than others. The area around the equator receives most energy. This region is hotter than elsewhere. The areas around the North and South Poles receive the least of the Sun's energy, and these areas are the coldest.

We saw on page 16 that heat flows from areas of high temperature to areas of low temperature. So heat moves from hotter regions towards colder ones. This heat flow produces ocean currents and winds.

Global winds

The uneven heating of the air is the driving force behind the prevailing (main) winds on Earth. If there were no complicating factors, there would be a giant **convection** current between the equator and each of the poles. Air is warmest at the equator so it rises, and flows towards the poles at high altitudes. Near the ground, colder air flows from the poles towards the equator.

AMAZING FACTS

Trade winds

Before the twentieth century, ships crossing the oceans relied on the wind to get them to their destination. The winds blowing from east to west around the equator were known as the trade winds. Ships sailing from Europe to America first sailed south, then picked up the trade winds for the passage west. On the return voyage ships travelled in the middle latitudes, where the winds blew mainly from west to east.

In fact, the flow of air is complicated by many factors. The main one is the rotation of the Earth. This breaks up the winds into three bands in each hemisphere – one close to the equator, one in the middle latitudes, and one near the poles. In each of these bands the wind is 'bent' by the Earth's rotation. The winds near the equator blow roughly from the east, while in the middle latitudes they blow roughly from the west. In the polar regions, the winds blow from the east. Over land, wind patterns are more complicated because local features such as mountain ranges affect the winds.

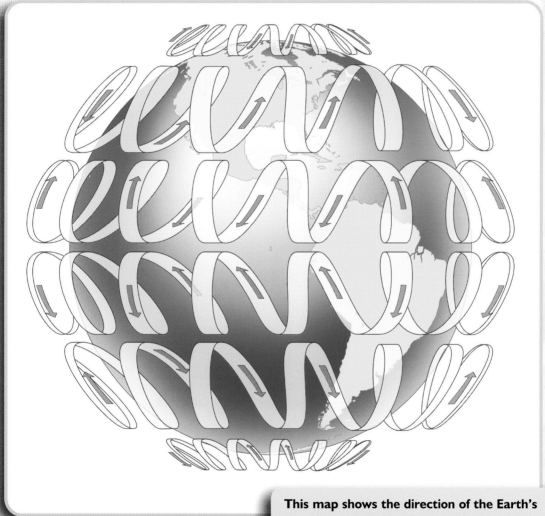

This map shows the direction of the Earth's prevailing winds. Bands of winds are separated by areas where there is little wind. The windless region around the equator is called 'the doldrums'.

Powering the weather

The winds, the Sun and the oceans between them are responsible for most of the weather around the world.

How warm or cold a place is depends mainly on how much sunlight it receives. Broadly, the closer a place is to the equator, the warmer its climate is.

The amount of rainfall a place receives relates to how far it is from the sea and the direction of the prevailing winds. The Sun's energy warms the oceans, and causes water from the ocean surface to evaporate (become gas) and rise into the air. Prevailing winds then carry the moist air until it is cooled in some way (for instance by rising over high ground). As the air cools, the water in it condenses (becomes liquid). At first the water forms tiny droplets that float through the air as clouds. However, as water droplets combine and get bigger, they become too heavy to float, and they fall as rain. If it is cold enough for the water to freeze, it may fall as snow or hail instead.

AMAZING FACTS

Energetic storms

It is not always obvious that the weather involves large amounts of energy. However, there is a great deal of power in a hurricane, as can be seen from the damage it can cause. The power used to sustain the rainfall in a hurricane for one day is 600,000 billion **watts**. This is 200 times the power output of all the power stations in the world!

From a satellite high above the Earth, the spiral shape of a hurricane can be seen clearly. The 'eye' at the centre, where there are no winds and the sky is clear, is a feature of any hurricane.

Ocean currents

Winds and uneven heating of the oceans together cause ocean currents. Heating causes water to expand, so at the equator the ocean surface is actually about 8 centimetres (3 inches) higher than at the poles. This slight difference makes the water tend to flow from the equator towards the poles. However, as with the winds, the Earth's rotation has an effect on the motion, as do the prevailing winds. The result is that at the surface, the ocean currents flow in great circles, known as gyres, around each **ocean basin**.

Ocean currents can have a large effect on the climate of land close by. Britain and western Europe have a much warmer climate than most other places at the same latitude because of the warming effects of the Gulf Stream, a warm current that flows across the Atlantic Ocean from the Gulf of Mexico, then runs north up the coast of western Europe.

This map shows the path of the Gulf Stream which starts in the Gulf of Mexico and runs across the Atlantic Ocean towards the coast of western Europe.

CHAPTER 8

Energy connections

Suppose you could follow a light beam as it arrived at the Earth's surface. From what we have already learned, there are many different things that could happen to the light energy. It could be absorbed by a rock, then radiate out again as **infra-red** radiation (heat). It could be absorbed by a leaf, converted into chemical energy and eventually become part of the plant. The plant could then be eaten by a herbivore, which could be eaten by a carnivore. The light beam could land on the ocean, and give some water enough energy to evaporate. Winds could then carry the moisture many kilometres before it falls as rain. Or the light could land on a solar cell and be converted into electricity. The electricity could be used to power a light bulb, and become light once again.

AMAZING FACTS

Dwarfing the Sun's energy

The amount of energy that a star produces is related to its brightness. The Sun is below average in terms of energy output. The brightest star in the sky, Sirius, is nearly 23 times brighter than the Sun. However, Sirius is over 500,000 times further from the Earth, so it shows only as a bright pinprick in the night sky. Other stars are even brighter than Sirius, but they do not shine so brightly in our night sky because they are even further away. Really giant stars can be several million times brighter than the Sun.

One of the stars in the constellation of Orion is known as the Pistol Star. It is about 10 million times brighter than the Sun, making it one of the brightest stars we know of. However, it is so far away that it is too faint to see without a telescope.

Transforming the Sun's energy

The many ways that energy from sunlight can be transformed illustrate just how much we rely on the Sun's energy. We have seen that energy generated in the rocks underground powers earthquakes and volcanoes, and the force of gravity can power a downhill bike ride. However, nearly every other kind of energy comes in one way or another from the Sun. The Sun's energy powers the winds, the weather and the movements of the oceans. Plants rely on sunlight for energy, and animals and other living things get their energy directly or indirectly from plants. Eighty-five per cent of the energy that humans use comes from fossil fuels, which are the remains of plants and animals made using the Sun's energy millions of years ago. Even **hydroelectricity** relies on energy from sunlight – if the Sun did not shine, all the water on Earth would be frozen as ice rather than flowing freely.

The Sun is the Earth's power station. Every form of energy on Earth ultimately comes from the Sun.

Energy in the future

Human energy needs are always increasing, and our main energy source (fossil fuels) is in limited supply. So what will we do for energy in the future? There are many different ideas. Energy production from **biomass** seems likely to increase, as will the energy from renewable sources and perhaps from nuclear power. There are also newer sources of energy that might be used.

This bus in Nebraska, USA, runs on soybean bio-diesel.

Fuel cells

A fuel cell is like a cross between a battery and an engine. Like an engine, it needs fuel to work (many fuel cells use hydrogen). However, a fuel cell does not burn its fuel. Instead, it uses it to make electricity, like a battery. Fuel cells can produce more power than batteries, and because they run on fuel they do not need recharging. Because they do not burn their fuel, they are more efficient than engines. A fuel cell using hydrogen as a fuel can be 80 per cent efficient. Fuel cells are already used to power artificial satellites and space probes as well as remote weather stations. Most cars that can run on more than one type of fuel have fuel cells.

 HYDROGEN ECONOMY

Hydrogen has a major advantage over fossil fuels – it produces only water when burned. Hydrogen can also be used to power fuel cells and make electricity. Unfortunately, at present hydrogen is made mainly from natural gas, a fossil fuel. There are many other ways of making hydrogen, the most promising of which is perhaps to make it from water. The hydrogen could then be used to produce energy when needed. The water produced when hydrogen is used as a fuel could be collected and converted into hydrogen once again.

Solar ideas

Solar energy supplies very little of our total energy at present, but there are several ways that this contribution could increase. Solar collectors, which gather the Sun's heat and use it to heat a liquid or power an engine, combined with solar cells generating electricity, could be used much more widely on houses and other buildings. In the future, satellites in space could collect solar energy and then beam it down to Earth using **microwaves**.

The initial costs of constructing a solar power satellite currently make this form of electricity far too expensive. However, newer, low-cost ways of getting into space may soon be available, and this could make a solar power satellite practical.

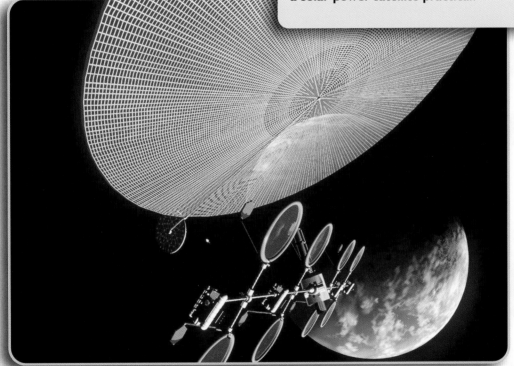

Nuclear fusion

Since the 1950s, scientists have been researching the use of **nuclear fusion** to produce energy. Nuclear fusion is the way that the Sun produces its energy. The process produces far more energy than **nuclear fission** (the way that current nuclear power stations produce energy). Furthermore, fusion does not produce dangerous **radioactive** wastes. Scientists have found ways to make fusion happen. However, so far the process uses nearly as much energy as it produces. There are many problems to be solved before fusion can become a useful source of energy.

Glossary

absolute zero the lowest possible temperature, exactly -273.16 °C, or -459.67 °F.

animal tissue group of similar cells, such as muscle.

atoms very tiny particles that make up all substances.

bacteria very tiny, simple micro-organisms (microscopic creatures).

biomass any material that comes originally from living things.

convection the movement of heat by circulation of air or water currents.

electromagnetic radiation any type of radiation with similar qualities to light, such as infra-red, ultraviolet, X-rays, microwaves and radio waves.

fermenting mixing substances with micro-organisms such as bacteria or yeasts in a warm environment with no air present.

filament in a light bulb, the filament is the very thin, tightly coiled wire that glows white-hot when the bulb is switched on.

friction a force between two objects rubbing against each other that resists the movement. Friction between two materials also generates heat.

global warming a gradual warming of the Earth's climate, which has been happening for the last 150 years or so.

hydroelectric power producing electricity using flowing water.

impermeable a substance that is impermeable does not allow liquid or gas to pass through it.

infra-red a kind of radiation, similar to light but invisible, which carries heat rather than light energy.

insulated protected from losing or gaining heat.

joule (J) the unit of measurement of energy. One J is the energy needed to move an object weighing 1 newton a distance of 1 metre.

kilocalorie (kcal) a unit used for measuring the amount of energy in food. A chocolate biscuit contains about 525 kcal of energy.

kilojoules (kJ) One kilojoule equals one thousand joules.

megajoules a million joules (J).

microwaves a type of electromagnetic radiation similar to radio waves. The energy of microwaves can be used to heat up living tissue.

molecule a combination of two or more atoms joined together by chemical bonds.

newton (N) the unit of measurement used to measure force. On Earth, a medium-sized apple weighs about 1 N.

nuclear fission a reaction involving the nucleus of an atom, in which uranium atoms are split into smaller atoms.

nuclear fusion a reaction involving the nucleus of an atom, in which hydrogen atoms fuse (join together) to form helium atoms.

ocean basin deep sections of the ocean, divided from each other by shallower areas called mid-ocean ridges.

radioactive a material that is radioactive gives out invisible, high-energy radiation. Radioactivity is harmful to humans.

reservoir an artificial lake made by damming a river.

sluice gates strong gates at the top of a water channel that control the flow along the channel.

watt (W) a measurement of power. One watt is the use of 1 joule of energy every second.

Further information

Books

The Energy Debate series. Wayland, 2007.

Eyewitness Science: Energy, Jack Challoner. Dorling Kindersley and Science Museum London, 1993.

Horrible Science: Killer Energy, Nick Arnold and Tony De Saulles. Scholastic Hippo, 2001.

Science Topics: Energy, Ann Fullick and Chris Oxlade. Heinemann Library, 1998.

Science Works: Energy, Steve Parker. MacDonald Young Books, 1995.

Young Oxford Library of Science: Energy and Forces, Neil Ardley. Oxford University Press, 2002.

Websites

Energy Quest
http://www.energyquest.ca.gov/
An excellent website from the California Energy Commission, with useful information, news, games and even a time machine!

BBC Bitesize revision
http://www.bbc.co.uk/schools/ks3bitesize/science/physics/energy_transfer_intro.shtml
A useful website setting out the essential information about energy resources and energy transformations.

Heat and temperature
http://www.sciencemuseum.org.uk/galleryguide/E3010.asp
A Science Museum website showing some of the early instruments used for measuring heat and temperature changes (including Joule's paddle-wheel apparatus).

PAC-Car II
http://www.paccar.ethz.ch/
More about the world's most efficient car

Web Weather for Kids
http://eo.ucar.edu/webweather/
Learn about hurricanes, tornadoes and try your hand at weather forecasting.

Extreme Science
http://www.extremescience.com/earthsciport.htm
Learn about plate tectonics, the biggest earthquakes and volcanoes, and some extreme weather.

Index